POSITIVE PRAYERS FOR CITIES

POSITIVE PRAYERS FOR CITIES

A RESOURCE FOR WORSHIP

BARBARA GLASSON

kevin
mayhew

kevin mayhew

First published in Great Britain in 2015 by Kevin Mayhew Ltd
Buxhall, Stowmarket, Suffolk IP14 3BW
Tel: +44 (0) 1449 737978 Fax: +44 (0) 1449 737834
E-mail: info@kevinmayhew.com

www.kevinmayhew.com

9 8 7 6 5 4 3 2 1 0

ISBN 978 1 84867 795 1
Catalogue No. 1501492

Cover design by Rob Mortonson
© Images used under licence from Shutterstock Inc.
Typeset by Melody-Anne Lee
Printed and bound in Great Britain

Contents

Foreword

Although I was born and brought up in the countryside, like most people I have lived significant parts of my life in and around cities. In the countryside I find an easy resonance with the God of creation and redemption, in the city I find the relationship more challenging. I have had to learn to love the city, and this requires a long-term commitment to her rhythms, nuances and nuisances.

The Methodist Church, in which I am a minister, like many other denominations, has often withdrawn from city centres and inner cities and found its home in the suburbs. This 'semi-detached' faith has often left us feeling negative about the humanly constructed environment. Cities can be viewed as hostile places and seemingly devoid of the Spirit of God. I am aware that riots and disturbances are often blamed on cities and can obscure the many creative things that happen.

I am conscious that many of the challenges of cities also extend to other urban areas. Towns and large estates often feel as though they have hard edges and more challenges than joys. I want to challenge us to think about the organic nature of our urban landscapes and to see them as places of growth and flourishing.

I have also wanted to discover a new language for the experience of being someone of faith in this variety of urban setting. I have looked for a gentler, more organic and affirming way to say what I see. In these poems and prayers I have also sought to discover the feminine attributes for the city, not through a token stab at inclusive language, but by addressing the city as if she is loved.

There are four main sections to this book, which I have named by liturgical colour, Purple, White, Red and Green. I hope this will enable suitable prayers for the time of year to be found with ease, or at the last minute before a service! At the end is a section titled 'Incarnation'. This is a gathering of prayers for particular people: surviving people, 'coming-out people', 'letting-go people', hopeful people. This section is a sort of pick-and-mix to dip into, as and when.

I have divided each of the main sections into adoration, confession, absolution, intercession, commitment and blessing so that they can be useful both in personal devotions and liturgical settings – as individual devotions or as part of public worship. It is meant to be the sort of book that you can just take off the shelf and find a way into your own prayer, as well as for more formal occasions

I hope that these prayers will give a starting point for a wider and deeper commitment to searching for God in our urban surroundings. I trust it will enable us to find the human face of God and be challenged to discover the city as holy ground.

See what you think!

About the author

Barbara Glasson is a Methodist minister and weaver who has spent most of her ministry in city centres, in particular Liverpool and Bradford. She is currently engaged in interfaith work in Bradford where she is team leader at Touchstone, a project working in partnership with Pakistan, supporting Christian communities and enhancing interfaith understanding both locally and internationally. Barbara has a particular engagement with the spirituality of adult survivors of childhood abuse. In all this work she is interested in how we 'hold it all together' both within ourselves and within communities and that has led her to consider what we understand by faith resilience and integrity.

Barbara Glasson's other publications for Kevin Mayhew are: *Finding a Way: Cutting-edge songs of seeking and searching* (3612537) and *Eating Curry for Heaven's Sake: Creative Christian interfaith engagement* (1501487). For further details, please see our website: www.kevinmayhew.com

Purple
Advent and Lent

In the church year, purple marks the time of waiting and mourning. We recall wilderness times as well as times of anticipation. What does this mean in the city, a place where Easter and Christmas are opportunities for marketing rather than for penance, and the creme egg follows the Christmas cracker without a pause?

In this section I have reflected on the mix of the city, the comings and goings, the migrations that happen on a daily and international basis. I have wanted to think about the ebb and flow of city life, the tastes and smells that permeate the air as the people of the city come and go.

I have imagined the city as a body, something that grows organically as well as structurally. This has helped me to think what incarnation means in the built environment, how we can plant our feet on the city's holy ground along with the incarnate God. How we learn to wait for what is unfolding around us.

Wistfully, I have mused on all the waiting that goes on within us and around us in the city environment, drawing together those who wait impatiently or anxiously for news or results with those for whom waiting is a way of life.

The final prayers in this section, look at purple as a royal colour, considering where power lies in the city and the Scriptural imperative that the first shall be last and the last first. The echoes of Christmas and Easter are around these prayers, but they try to hold back on celebration in an attempt to acknowledge the intensity of waiting that the city presents and the anticipation or terror of the purple times.

Starting over

Adoration

The city is putting on a fresh face,
she has pasted posters on her billboards
and her streets are clean.

The city is dressed differently today,
she has flung wide her heaviest shutters,
her windows glinting.

The city is waking in a new light,
she has brushed her steps,
drawn out her awnings,
her tables are spread.

The city is wearing her dancing shoes,
she is bountiful, bursting with colour,
her arms wide open.

Confession

Why is it hard to forget the past?
Why is it hard to be assured?
Why is it hard to fret less for tomorrow?
Why is it hard to play our part?

When will we stop begrudging sorrows?
When will we stop resisting pain?
When will we stop rehearsing grudges?
When will we stop shutting the door?

How long will we continue falling?
How long will we always mess things up?
How long will it take to learn the lesson?
How long will we keep on losing heart?

Absolution   We are indeed free to live our questions
without fear,
we are indeed free to name our doubts
without shame,
we are indeed free to let go of the past,
we are indeed free.
Thank God for that!

Intercession   In the regeneration of the city:
if we have mistaken questionnaires
for consultation;
confused surveys with dialogue;
been led more by planners than by passion;
then we ask God to show us a better way.

If we have raised some at the expense of others;
or set up unfair competition within our region;
been led more by greed than neighbourliness;
then we ask God to show us a better way.

If we have spoken in jargon at the expense of
the truth;
sold new ideas to safeguard personal interests;
been led by profit margins rather than
social inclusion;
then we ask God to show us a better way.

If we have changed the city superficially
and quickly;
looked more for a hasty fix than lasting
transformation;
been led by shallow appearance rather than
important values;
then we ask God to show us a better way.

If we have favoured the powerful at the expense
of the poorest;
sanitised the city and excluded those who do
not conform;
been led more by an agenda of safety than one
of flourishing;
then we ask God to show us a better way.

If we have demolished heritage of the city in our
hurry to make all things new;
disregarded the stories of local people and
bulldozed memories;
been led more by grand designs than a sense
of place;
then we ask God to show us a better way.

Remind us, God, that regeneration is not the same
as resurrection,
that your desire for the city is that it should have
heart and life.
That we should look to the good of all people,
not just elites
and that the city of God can never be constructed
by power
but only by the long-term commitment
of vulnerable love.

Commitment   Whenever it is tough,
we will continue.
Whenever hearts are broken,
we will warm.

Whenever thoughts are rigid,
we will challenge.
Whenever discouraged,
we will pray.

Whoever goes with us,
we will embolden.

Whoever deserts us,
we will bless.

Whoever is friendly,
we will embrace kindly.
Whatever it costs us,
we will pay.

Wherever God sends us,
we will go gladly.
Wherever God finds us,
we will keep heart.

Wherever God guides us,
we will walk gently.
Wherever God takes us,
we will stay.

Blessing   May the God of Abraham and Sarah, who took
people out of exile and led them to a land of
promise,
give us the perseverance and resilience to live in
our city,
and in all things may we trust God's provision of
mercy, tenacity and love,
which has been unfailingly provided from one
generation to another
and continually restores the peoples of the earth.
Amen.

Migration

Adoration

Flying overhead,
starlings swirl to roost,
the river ebbs
and flows.

Apple lassi chilled,
curried lamb with chips,
Halal tagine
and rice.

Merlot Sauvignon,
Kentish vin de table,
Scotch from Japan
and ice.

Starlings swirl up high,
rivers flow and ebb,
tide washes in
and goes.

People roost and swirl,
some just scraping by,
perch for a while
and fly.

Confession

Exodus God,
who has left the place of security
to be a migrant in this alien world,
we confess that we have been so preoccupied
with our need to belong
that we have overlooked those with no
abiding city
and that we have become territorial
concerning your love.

Help us, who feel increasingly invaded
by those from outside,
to be so hospitable to the incomers in our cities
that we become transformed in our souls
and hearts,
finding your promise fulfilled
amongst the stranger, the newcomer and the
migrant worker,
so that we may find a new community
of peace and hope together.

Absolution   Remember that you are also guests in this
perplexing world;
recall the intentions of my kingdom
where there are neither territories nor possessions;
revisit the gentle persuasion of my love
to be at home within my promise.

Pilgrim people,
you will find your rest in me!

Intercession   Restless God,
we pray for everyone who is unsettled:
for gypsies by blood or persuasion,
for those who have no home,
for people who cannot rest,
hear our prayer.

Restless God,
we pray for everyone who is unsettling:
for the troubled,
for those who are not at home in their own heads,
for people who cannot rest,
hear our prayer.

Restless God,
we pray for everyone who is unsettled:
for the migrants,
for those who have been trafficked for
their bodies,
for people who cannot rest,
hear our prayer.

Restless God,
we pray for everyone who is unsettling:
for asylum seekers,
for those who fear the knock of dawn raids,
for people who cannot rest,
hear our prayer.

Restless God,
we pray for everyone who is unsettled:
for people with disability,
for those whose pain causes long, sleepless nights,
for people who cannot rest,
hear our prayer.

Commitment   I pledge
that I will not rest
until all God's people
are sheltered in this place.

I pledge
that I will journey
until all divisions
disintegrate and fall.

I pledge
that I will travel
until the waters part
to feel God's promised grace.

I pledge
that I will not settle
until this city space
brings all within her walls.

Blessing God of all journeys,
travel with us,
so that we may envisage
a land of belonging and promise.
Bring us eventually
to a resting place,
so that we may abide gladly
within your citadel of love.
Amen.

Body

Adoration

I see red tankers,
smell pumping petrol,
taste gas vapours,
feel energy,
hear power.

I hear fan outlets,
see hot air rising,
feel the outflows,
taste the pressure,
smell steam.

I taste sweeper dust,
see the cleansed gutters,
hear the brushes,
smell the dry leaves,
feel clean.

I smell bakeries,
feel the memories,
hear the laughter,
taste the yeast scent,
see smiles.

I feel the city,
smell new potential,
hear of openings,
see my chances,
taste life.

Confession

Trouble is, we have approached the city
like a structure
and not a human dwelling place.

Trouble is, we have treated the urban
environment like an object
and abused our shared space.

Trouble is, we have related to each other
with arrogance
and forgotten our common humanity.

Trouble is, we have viewed the streets as hostile
and overlooked our mutual responsibility.

Trouble is, we have given others status
and been unconcerned with challenging injustice.

Trouble is, we have forgotten that God was
crucified in a city
and continued to overwhelm each other
with power.

Trouble is, we have made the city in our image
and not lived well enough to declare it good.

Absolution Trouble is, we have forgotten just how much God
loves the city
and that Jesus was not only condemned but
raised there.
We are now free to see things with fresh eyes
and to live as people of continuing resurrection.
Trouble is calmed by forgiveness and we are
forgiven!
Alleluia!

Intercession Loving God, who is not only distant
but also earthed,
we pray that those with power in our city
will also keep their feet on the ground.

Loving God, who is not only creator
but also embodied,
we pray that those with gifts in our city
will remember the dispossessed.

Loving God, who is not only crucified
but also raised,
we pray that those who suffer neglect in our city
will also experience new possibility.

Loving God, who is not only all compassionate
but also wounded,
we pray that those who suffer violence in our city
will also hear the news of peace.

Loving God who is not only ascended
but also returning,
we pray that we may be so committed to our city
that we can be messengers of heaven.

Loving God, who is not only the Alpha but also
the Omega,
both the beginning and the end,
we pray that, whilst on earth, we the city people
will have the perspective of eternity.

Commitment

I will put my body where my beliefs are,
I will plant my feet on the city's holy ground.
I will breathe only for God,
I will walk in God's ways.

I will stand in this city rejoicing,
I will keep God's promise in my heart.
I will breathe only for God,
I will walk in God's ways.

I will walk these streets with gladness,
I will swing my arms in praise.
I will breathe only for God,
I will walk in God's ways.

I will bear the city's sorrow,
I will cry tears of longing and lament.
I will breathe only for God,
I will walk in God's ways.

For you are the God of Jerusalem,
the one whose body is love-broken.
I will breathe only for God,
I will walk in God's ways.

My body is the temple of the incarnate God,
I will place myself at the city's heart.
I will breathe only for God,
I will walk in God's ways.

Blessing   Bless to us good God,
our legs and feet,
our beating hearts,
our inner parts,
our city street.
Amen.

Waiting

Adoration

Praise be to God for all who wait:
for those who let us off the bus,
for those who stand with us at crossings,
for those who queue.

Praise be to God for all waitresses:
for the menus they bring,
for the right food to the right table,
for their attention to our needs.

Praise be to God for all waiting rooms:
for the distractions and comforts,
for receptionists and appointments,
for knowing our turn will come.

Praise be to God the waiter:
for hearing us,
for serving us,
for feeding us.

Confession

Forgive me God,
that my feet tap
more from impatience
than from catching the beat.

Forgive me God,
that my fingers strum
more from irritation
than from playing the tune.

Forgive me God,
that my tongue tutts
more from disapproval
than from singing the song.

Forgive me God,
that my legs pace
more from anxiety
than from joining the dance.

Absolution   Waiting God, bring me
to find the rhythm in stillness,
to find the music in silence,
to find the holding in openness,
to find the centre in edginess,
to find the possibility in pausing,
to find absolution in waiting.

Intercession   I hold before God
and in my heart
those who wait to be born
and those who wait to give birth.

I hold before God
and in my heart
those who wait for tests
and those who wait for results.

I hold before God
and in my heart
those who wait for chances
and those who wait for work.

I hold before God
and in my heart
those who wait to die
and those who wait to release them.

I hold before God
and in my heart
those who wait to be born
and those who wait to receive them.

Commitment   When the city hems me in
I commit myself to three deep breaths:
one for patience,
one for wisdom,
one for love.

When the kids are full of beans
I commit myself to three deep breaths:
one for patience,
one for wisdom,
one for love.

When the boss gives me no credit
I commit myself to three deep breaths:
one for patience,
one for wisdom,
one for love.

When my partner does it again
I commit myself to three deep breaths:
one for patience,
one for wisdom,
one for love.

When my mother drives me crazy
I commit myself to three deep breaths:
one for patience,
one for wisdom,
one for love.

When I think I'm really useless
I commit myself to three deep breaths:
one for patience,
one for wisdom,
one for love.

Blessing   Waiting God,
bless our city
with patience,
our streets with kindness,
our hearts with merriment,
our hopes with love.

Royalty

Adoration

God of mysterious majesty,
whose signature authorises the universe,
who decrees the realm of peace:

we praise you for the cityscape,
for domes and turrets,
oratories and obelisks,
for towers that prod the heavens,
the proportions of pillars,
the acoustics of concert halls,
the resonance of marble,
the grandeur of granite.

Reign as sovereign in this place,
so that we, the nonconformists,
can solely honour your authority:
the authority of grace;
the authority of compassion;
the authority of the poor.

Confession

We confide in Jesus:
policies that exclude the struggling;
policing that assumes stereotypes;
politicians that court only re-election.

We confide in Jesus:
corruption of good intentions;
cynicism at the expense of compassion;
controls that seek only civil compliance.

We confide in Jesus:
interest rates that compound debt;
vested interests that line rich pockets;
disinterest in the needs of the poorest.

Absolution
We confide all this in Jesus,
the donkey-riding King,
confident in his ability to turn the tables
on all that corrupts, undermines or
underestimates
the coming of the realm of love.

Intercession
God who stirred a patriarch
to loosen his tent pegs,
God who asked a queen
to adopt an unknown child,
God who caused a king
to read the writing on the wall,
God who called the Magi
to bow before a baby:
may all principalities and fiefdoms,
all politicians and patriarchs,
all dynasties and dictatorships,
all princes and presidents,
all highnesses and lord lieutenants,
all royalties and rajas,
all sultans, and Sufis,
all sirs and sheikhs,
all principals and powers,
kneel at the stable door
robed in humility,
read the signs of the times
titled with lowliness,
lead civic processions
crowned with contrition,
embody the freedom of the city
dubbed with love.

Commitment

I dream of a right royal garden party
where no one needs a hat
or even a napkin,
in which the drifters and addicts
are invited from the highways to the
highest table.

I dream of food for everyone,
not cream cakes and scones
but a feast wholesome and sustaining,
a meal to simple tastes, filling each soul to
the brim.

I dream of an etiquette of acceptance,
where rough stories can be heard,
not with judgement but with understanding
and the attention deep enough to be cut with
a knife.

I dream of the poorest at the prince's elbow
and the queen waiting on their needs,
not with reluctance but generously providing
a spread fit for a king.

I dream of abundance, a cup running over,
an occasion of deep-bellied laughter,
a place where grace is not only spoken but lived,
a blessing of bounty.

I dream of a bread-breaking table,
where the wine of sadness is poured out
amongst us,
and the exquisite intensity of joy is not
rationed
but drenched into our bowls.

Blessing	May this city be approached
by the prince on the donkey,
may this city be entered
by the table-turning king,
may this city be occupied
by the insurgence of justice,
may this city be governed
by the rule of integrity,
may this city be judged
by the reign of understanding,
may this city be ruled
by the power of hope.

White
Christmas and Easter

In this section I have begun to think about the city as a place of the bearing of God, the place where God is coming to birth on a daily basis, amongst the ordinary events around us. I have considered how the city is blessed by the presence of the Spirit, amongst the struggles that are prevalent in the urban context, and I have prayed that we will greet something else at the centre of it all.

I have also focused on the mixed blessing of Christmas, how it sets the city alight but also brings fear and anxiety for many. Maybe it's best summed up in the words of absolution, 'It's ok: Christmas passes, Christ endures'.

In writing these 'white' prayers, I have continually delved into the ordinary city places and tried to discover in them the colour and texture of the incarnate presence of God. I have continually been surprised by evidence of the Almighty amongst the ordinary, and in the spaces that the city affords for stillness and life. In calling the richness of such incarnation to mind, there has been a new sense of God impregnated in the life around us and the possibility of transformation from within the cityscape.

This transformative potential gives a sense that God works from the inside out, that the urban context is changed by the small, often unnoticed events that unfold each day. As a barrel of flour is raised by the hidden yeast, so the day-to-day round of city life is made subtly and significantly different by this working of God within it. I have been able to call to mind the ordinary people that transform my life –

the milkman, the cleaners, lift engineers, workmen and women and night watchmen – and give thanks in a new way. This feels like a daily blessing of ordinary things.

Finally, I have been drawn into the story of the 'Prodigal Son', in which I have heard a new resonance of God's longings, not just of individuals but also for the built environment. I have written prayers for missing people, for travellers, wanderers, the forgotten and the homesick. I have been drawn into a new commitment to be passionate about all the people of the city, especially those who are easily overlooked.

Bearing

Adoration

I greet the divine essence of this day.
I greet the silence that hangs on the coat tails
of dawn.
I greet the rising of the sun behind the domes,
the circling of the gulls above the chimney stacks.

Good morning blessed city,
good morning to your cracks and crookedness,
good morning to your bricks and brokenness,
I greet the silent lions on your plinths.

I find you sleep worn, rubbing the road dust from
your shuttered eyes,
I find you tipsy with morning, teetering across
the slabs and shiny slates,
I find you as empty as a picked pocket,
bereft and full of fluff,
you are top heavy with daylight, you are awake.

I greet the divine essence of you,
your reputation as smeared as lipstick
on twice-kissed lips,
your brashness, your hip-held hand,
bearing witness,
bearing testimony,
bearing Christ.

Confession

If I have not passed praise when praise is bound,
if I have not put blame where blame is due,
if I have not given pause to fleeting thought,
if I have not searched out where truth is found,
if I have not respected the inner child,
if I have not trusted the heart's desire,
if I have not seen the matter through,
if I have not been burnt by the Spirit's fire,

if I have not pondered a better way,
if I have not taken a different road,
if I have not learned a lesson taught,
if I have not listened but had my say,
if I have carried too heavy a load,
as if God's love could bear no shame:

then let me lay this sadness down,
then let me lay this sadness down,
then let me lay this sadness down,
and let me start my life again.

Absolution
To be free is to be released from all the 'what ifs'
of the past
and released into the anticipation of the future.
Such freedom is God's intention for our lives,
that we can flourish into new possibilities,
new joys, new adventures, new hopes.
We are made within the imagination of the
Divine,
we are crafted for enjoyment and delight;
this is not ours by virtue,
but simply as gift.
Alleluia!

Intercession
When we are browbeaten, bothered or stuck,
may we greet something else at the centre of it all;
when we are disappointed, disheartened
or down,
may we greet something else at the centre of it all;
when we are discredited, dishonoured or in debt,
may we greet something else at the centre of it all;
when we are compassion-weary or overly cynical,
may we greet something else at the centre of it all;

when we assume things, or people, or life in
general are just rubbish,
may we greet something else at the centre of it all.

We bring our turmoil to the centring of Christ,
we bring our troubles to the centring of the Spirit,
we bring our torments to the centring of God.

Bring us to our depths, to our essence,
to our hearts,
to discover you at the centre of all that is,
and all that is yet to be revealed.

Commitment As people of this place,
we commit ourselves to:
living more openly;
going more gently;
finding more beauty;
trusting more profoundly;
forgiving more sincerely;
thinking more deeply;
being more godly;
because of Jesus,
the way, the truth and the life.

Blessing May we greet our city as if an angel
disguised as a stranger.
Amen.

Incarnation

Adoration

The city is adorned
like a bride for her husband,
she is sparkled
like the light in an eye,
she wears garlands
across her roads,
she is as gifted
as a dancer.

The city is laden
like an ass on a journey,
she is tinselled
like the gold in a chest,
she wears frost
on her windows,
she is as jewelled
as a princess.

The city is expectant
like a child on her birthday,
she is treasured
like a babe in a cot,
she wears gladness
in her street songs,
she is as star-bright
as an angel.

Confession

For hating Christmas,
for dreading Christmas,
for fearing Christmas,
for ruining Christmas,
forgive me God.

For the reasons behind the hating, the dreading,
the fearing and the ruining,
please bring insight, wisdom, understanding and
the healing of bad memories.

Absolution It's ok:
Christmas passes,
Christ endures.

Intercession As a mother holds the moment,
as a father holds her hand,
as a star holds our attention,
as a Christmas meal is planned.

As a hen gathers her chickens,
as the children take a turn,
as a healing of a friendship,
as a prodigal returns.

As the setting of a table,
as a joke that makes no sense,
as the tending of a shepherd,
Christmas in the present tense.

As the strangers who are angels,
as the fielding of the sheep,
as wine is poured from water,
as a stance that holds the peace.

May this day be full and hearty,
may you find the ways to cope,
may your soul be still and gentle,
may Christmas Day hold you in hope.

Commitment   God of Bethlehem,
I ask for grace to find you present
behind the walls of troubles
which separate me from my kin
and in all these things
I pray that you will strengthen me
to see the world with fresh eyes,
to find you beside me and beyond me,
to continue to believe
that you are incarnate,
both in this place and in my heart.

Blessing   May the same Jesus, who came to the city
to be counted,
be so present for you, around you and within you
that you know your true value and worth.
Amen.

Courting

Adoration Enter his gates with thanksgiving and his courts with praise.

In the courtyards of this city I give praise to God:
with thanksgiving for the spaces they afford,
with gratitude for their respite from making choices,
with relief as I rest my body from so much carrying.

In the food courts of this city I give praise to God:
with amazement at the variety of delicious produce,
with astonishment at the enterprise that provisions the world,
with wonder at colour and texture that stock the shelves.

In the sports courts of this city I give praise to God:
with joy at the vigour of lively competitors,
with admiration at the vitality of exuberant play,
with awe at the disciplined training of energetic bodies.

In the forecourts of the city I give praise to God:
with patience for those who anticipate trains,
with excitement as coaches release their passengers,
with solidarity with all who have missed their connections.

In the law courts of this city I give praise to God:
with honour for the people that face accusers,
with respect for the law makers and upholders,
with tenderness for the battered and belligerent.

I enter the gates of this city with thanksgiving and into its courtyards with praise.

Confession I have to confess there are times when I lose
patience with this city,
with the revolving-door offenders, the petty
nuisances.
I confess to being caught in cycles of anger caused
by the people in my way
or who slow me down when I am being
single-minded.

I have to confess that I can too easily become one
of a crowd
and get caught up in things that I wouldn't do if
it was left to me.
I confess to following the person who stirs
things up
or whose actions provoke a response in me that is
ill-tempered or mean.

I have to confess that this city can bring out the
worst in me,
with its restrictions and regulations, surveillance
cameras and patrols.
I confess to being caught out by the seductions
of consumerism
or to driving bargains that are exploitative
of others.

I have to confess that I have used the city like a
personal service,
expecting it to be constantly replenished to fulfil
my needs.
I confess that I have courted my own desires at
the expense of others
or have felt cheated when I have not quickly got
what I want.

I have to confess that I have been neglectful of
God in the city,
assuming that the things of faith are domestic
and homely, not urban and edgy.
I confess to being caught up with my own
thoughts and needs
or being neglectful of the city as civic community
and holy ground.

I have to confess that I have struggled to love
this city in all its complexity,
preferring neat solutions to struggling with the
nuance and contradiction it presents.
I confess to often being caught between
secularism and simplistic religion
or to being more preoccupied with finding
solutions than living the challenges the
city presents.

Absolution Even as we confess our failure, we see that our
vulnerability is also our strength,
whilst we engage with the world, we are both
troubled and redeemed,
at the same time as acknowledging our struggles,
we participate in change,
so confession and absolution are not opposites,
but two sides of the same coin
and in this is hope, not just for us but for the
whole world.

Intercession   Walk with us, God, through the trials of this city.

We pray for all accusers
and for the accused.
We pray for all adjudicators
and the judged.
We pray for all key holders
and those locked in.
We pray for all who serve time
and those with time to spend.

Walk with us, God, through the trials of this city.

We pray for all abandoned
and for the fearful.
We pray for all defendants
and those who wash their hands.
We pray for those who plead
and those who remain silent.
We pray for those convicted
and those who have been betrayed.

Walk with us, God, through the trials of this city.

We pray for all victims
and for their supporters.
We pray for all who have experienced abuse
and for those violated by violence.
We pray for all who tell the truth
and those who hear the evidence.
We pray for those who suffer innocently
and for those whose guilt is crucifying them.

Walk with us, God, through the trials of this city;
bring us a new freedom, we pray.

Commitment   We commit ourselves to open-handedness,
not tight-fistedness,
we commit ourselves to opening doors,
not locking them,
we commit ourselves to giving, not thieving,
we commit ourselves to honesty, not deception.

We commit our city to the way of Jesus,
the man who, when committed to death because
of others' fear,
opened his arms in commitment to the world,
through love.

Blessing   May the God of mercy
set the city free.
Amen.

Inside out

Adoration

Thanks be to God for all small city places,
for changing rooms, benches, more seats on
the bus,
stock rooms, staff lounges, settees made
of leather,
street angels, park wardens, policemen in pairs.

Thanks be to God for all foyers and porches,
for doorsteps and pavements and toilets
that flush,
rooms to change babies, crèches to play in,
bandstands, umbrellas and travelling fairs.

Thanks be to God for time out of the weather,
for hairdressers, bookstalls to browse
without rush,
cafes with awnings, car parks with spare spaces,
cubicles, markets and places for prayers.

Thanks be to God for night porters with torches,
for museums, galleries, library's hush,
shelters on platforms, taxis, hotel rooms,
chairs in hall lobbies and landings on stairs.

Confession

When we overlook the small to court the mighty,
when we underrate the fragile to acquire the
upper hand,
when we live inside our heads to outsmart our
heart's imperatives,
when we overwhelm the voiceless to make sure
we say our piece,
when we assume we cannot change things
to avoid some hard decisions,
when we undervalue self to defer to
market forces,

when we are neglectful of our blessings to
reinforce our prejudice,
upside-down God,
forgive us.

Turn us round, God,
shake us up, God,
take us in, God,
push us out, God,
inside-out God,
upside-down God,
forgive us.

Absolution   In the city of God
the first are last
and the last first.
This is both our judgement
and our salvation.

Intercession   To God I bring the street in which I live:
the people who stand on my doorstep each day,
unseen deliverers of milk,
leaflets, letters and newspapers.
To Jesus I bring the people who live beside me,
and underneath and overhead and across
the street.

To God I bring all shelf stackers, caretakers
and night watchmen,
lavatory attendants, cleaners and lift engineers,
all who attend to the city's needs unnoticed.
To Jesus I bring everyone that drops in,
everyone that drops out,
everyone that calls in
and everyone that calls out.

To God I bring the burrowers,
drivers of diggers and dumper trucks,
those who trace cables or broken drains,
the menders and minders of roads.
To Jesus I bring all borrowers,
beggars and seekers of refuge,
the terrorised, the terrorist and the terror-struck.

To God I bring everyone that attends to me,
also everyone whose hanging around or banging
or bustling or leaflet drops annoy me,
asking that the tables of this city will be turned,
so that those who consider themselves last
will be first
and those that consider themselves first
will not last!

Commitment   In God's name I commit myself:
to taking more notice,
to thinking more kindly,
to being more grateful.
In Jesus' name I commit myself:
to taking less umbridge,
to thinking less meanly,
to being less greedy.
In the city's name I commit myself:
to taking less readily,
to thinking more closely,
to judging less quickly.

Blessing   A blessing on all overlooked people.
A blessing on all taken-in people.
A blessing on all shouting-out people.
A blessing on all churning-round people.
A blessing on all shaken-up people.
A blessing on all turning-about people.
Amen.

A place of prodigality

Adoration

Thanks be to you,
waiting God,
who stands at the threshold
of all that is possible
and holds fast in steadfast hope.

We praise you for the perseverance
of your love,
for the unbounded expectation
of your promise,
for the encompassing
of your far-reaching gaze.

We thank you that you have found us
amongst the odd, the troubled and the unlikely
and that in the finding
you have embraced all that is possible
within us, through us and despite us.

You are the God of all homecomings,
who questions not where we have been,
or what we have done,
or why we have left
but only why it took us so long to return.

Confession

I am footloose and you steadfast,
I am waster and you creator,
I am loser and you provider,
I am feckless and you faithful,
I am restless and you tireless,
I am reckless and you rooted,
I am the prodigal child of the prodigal city.

Absolution   God says:
I am waiting and longing,
I am generous and gentle,
I am steady and stable,
I am firm-rooted and steady,
I am the Father of all that is lost.

You are ready to come home,
you are ready to be received home,
I am ready to welcome you home,
I am home.
Thanks be!

Intercession   I pray this day for the lost ones:
for missing persons,
for those who are missing them.
For those who are out of their mind,
for those who are minding them.
For travellers, wanderers and rootless people,
for those who stay grounded for them.
For the homesick,
for those who are sick of home.

I pray this day for the unnamed ones:
for those who are forgotten,
for those who have forgotten.
For those who try to forget,
for those who fear to remember.
For the forgetful,
for those who recollect them.
For the remiss, remorseful and resentful,
for those who remind them of many things.

I pray this day for the waiting ones:
for the wakeful nights,
for the waiting days.
For the prisoners of poverty,
for the free and easy.

For those who try to go back,
for those who fear to go forward.
For the misfits, the mystics and the misguided,
for all those who love us anyway.

Commitment   If I can commit myself to cry tears of rage,
if I can commit myself to shed tears of empathy,
if I can commit myself to dry tears of frustration,
if I can commit myself to laugh tears of
unbounded joy,
before anything is resolved or fixed or sorted,
then I bring the salt of my tears to this city.

If I can cry out at acts of violence,
if I can cry out at signs of neglect,
if I can cry out when the precious are broken,
if I can cry out with heartfelt delight,
before anything is finished or tidied
or judged,
then I place my crying into the wailing wall
of this city.

If I can ache for things to be different,
if I can ache for things changing over,
if I can ache for someone to notice,
if I can ache for sheer merriment in the face
of the absurd,
before anything is clear or explained or better,
then I carry this ache with me, bearing the hope
of transformation into this city.

I commit myself to the crying,
I commit myself to the laughing,
I commit myself to the hoping,
I commit myself to the noticing,
I commit myself to this city,
I commit myself to God's city.

Blessing   God who risked his inheritance on both prodigal
and stay-at-home:
bless the wasters and workers,
bless the sleepers and wakers,
bless the drifters and workers,
bless the losers and shakers.
Amen.

Red
Passion and Pentecost

Red is the colour of the Spirit, that blows across the city and brings life and passion. In these prayers I imagine the Spirit's work amongst the stories of the city, the yarns and memories that are shared in cafes and bars, the nostalgia of the elderly and the exuberance of the young. I think about how stories emerge and how they are shared, how the very stones of the city would cry out if they could, to tell of the history that is buried beneath and contained within the walls of the buildings and streets. I also reflect on an experience I had at Leeds station and pray for all people who have been silenced or demeaned.

I reflect on the promises that people make to the city, in regeneration schemes and public policy and I think of the promises that God makes, the covenant relationship that sustains us within the cityscape. I dream of a new city, one where shanties are replaced with good houses and everything is made better than new. I pray to the adventurous God who lends us the city in a covenant of grace, asking that we will embody a new relationship between earth and heaven.

These prayers also consider the place of strangers in the city, for the small kindnesses that surround us each day amongst unknown passengers on the free city bus, or asylum support service. I remember incomers, immigrants and insurgents, refugees and gypsies and some who are strangers to themselves.

I reflect on how the Spirit fills the city with new possibility, and try to counter the tendency we have to be cynical. I pray that the city will rise to new heights and be transformed by the risen Christ. That we will be surprised by possibilities and curious about what the future may hold.

Finally I have reflected on how rage and anger can be transformed in an urban context, and how the energy of the spirit is a countersign to the energy of destruction. I long for us to stand in solidarity with all that is broken and to be signs of resistance and hope. I pray that the God of wrath and righteousness will fill the city with holy anger, tempered with mercy.

Storyteller

Adoration

From boundaries to roof tops
the city spins her yarns,
sharpened flints mark her foundations,
shards of pot, corroded coins tell her tales.
Her doorsteps are scored by pilgrim feet,
her storylines, like wrinkles on her facades.

She is hallmarked with history, declared
and silent,
from her blue plaques to her graffiti subways.
She is our grandmother on whose knee we ride,
at times talkative, garrulous, nostalgic,
a raconteur of family folklore, etched on
gravestones,
marking time on low lintels.

Her rivers are deep with memories,
remembering migration, forced and chosen,
their banks, rippling, wave handkerchiefs,
lapping up reunions,
pulling the generations this way and that.

Her sunken cobbles have rattled, like the tut
of a tongue,
to the horse-drawn hearse,
the wooden baby carriage,
trams, hansom cabs,
the clop of clogs and hooves,
heard the pad of bare feet and clack of
platform soles.

Siren city, you have lured the workers to their
morning shifts,
whispered secrets in their ears like a temptress.
If these stones could cry aloud, we would
hear hosannas,
psalms of sadness, testaments to endurance.

Confession

Once upon a time there was a station,
and in that station there was a platform,
and the platform number was 12B.

On platform 12B stood a lawyer in his warm
worsted jacket,
a group of teachers at the end of term
and a priest returning from London.

Beside them all a mother with her daughter,
the daughter's name was Sarah
and her mother was spitting in Sarah's face.

The mother told Sarah that she was rubbish,
the mother told Sarah that she was evil,
the mother told Sarah that she would not
have Christmas.

The lawyer looked at the priest and raised
his eyes,
the teachers shuffled in case they were needed
and the priest rested her weight on one leg
because she was so tired.

The mother dragged Sarah by her coat's
furry hood,
she pushed her up the stairs,
she screamed at her over and over,
the sound was masked by the arrival of the train
on platform 12B.

The lawyer and the priest and the teachers got
onto the train,
they shook their heads, they hunched
their shoulders,
they tried to think up a happy ending.

If only this was a fairy tale.
(I confess, that I was the priest.)

Absolution

For all the times we simply haven't known
what to do,
we ask for forgiveness.
In God's imagination the story of redemption
is told over and over,
we are made in God's imagination,
we can be different.

Intercession

Remembering the times we have not challenged
violent behaviour,
we pray for people who are abused,
silenced or demeaned.

Remembering the times that we have made
assumptions because of racial difference,
we pray for people who are not seen to be unique
or individual.

Remembering the times we have not known how
to open up conversations,
we pray for people who are never listened to
or heard.

Remembering the times when we have perceived
the city to be inevitably hostile,
we pray for people who are committed to giving
her a human face.

Remembering the times we have behaved as
observers in life rather than participants,
we pray for people who put themselves at risk
to make a difference.

Remembering the stories of the city,
we pray that we will become more attentive,
more fearless, more compassionate.
We ask our prayers in the name of Jesus,
who in the city was both victim and redeemer.

Commitment In the stories of Jesus
there were people who wanted to throw stones,
who were untouchable,
who demanded attention,
who climbed trees to keep out of the way.
There were also people who were drawn in,
who were healed,
who stopped and got involved,
who listened and were changed.
We commit ourselves to living these stories,
as participants, not bystanders.

Blessing Storyteller God,
bless our listening outwards,
bless our listening inwards,
bless our listening downwards,
bless our listening upwards.
Amen.

Promise

Adoration

I saw a new city, because the old one had been
swept away,
a holy place fit for a king.
There was a red carpet rolled out for the beggars
and they were no longer in pain.

The old city had been banished by the sea,
the shanties were replaced by good houses
and God was present in the rebuilding,
everything was made better than new.

God promised to live in this city,
so that the anguish and lament
could be washed clean,
not by tears, but by life-giving water.

A new order shone like a lamp, as bright
as a jewel
and mercy was the measuring cup for justice.
This new-found city was burnished with mercy,
with the names of the righteous written on
its streets.

Confession

Dear City,
I am writing this note to say that many things
have come to my attention that, I consider, are far
from perfect.

Let us begin with the litter, the disregard for the
environment, the dog mess and vomit on the
pavement. Then let us look deeper: you have
neglected to notice the lonely, the displaced
and the despondent that trudge up and down
your streets. Worse than that, you have turned
your back on human values, assuming that you

are powerless to make any changes and shrugged your shoulders at the future.

Please make sure you mend your ways.

Yours sincerely,
Me

Dear You,
I am sorry that you have put the blame on me, for what is our shared responsibility.

You have made me, so why don't you consider me to be any good?

Can I remind you that if you want change, you need to start honouring your part of the bargain? After all, we are together in this thing, inextricably linked.

Yours as ever,
The City

Absolution Dear Both,

We live in this place together; I have after all, become incarnate in your mess.

The good news is, we can make it different – together that is. Looking forward to the partnership.

Yours faithfully,
God

Intercession Loving God,
we pray for the city,
whose promises are often squandered
for cheap rewards.
We pray for all people whose prospects appear
unpromising
and who have lost trust in the system.

We pray for the victims of broken promises
who so often feel betrayed and discarded.
We pray for those who live on promises
or the never-never.

Loving God,
you have made a covenant with the city
and you dream of a place of equity and trust.
May we, who know the promise of resurrection,
be bearers of practical help
and honest friendship
so that our transactions may be for the
common good
and honour the vision of a lasting kingdom.

Commitment Adventurous God,
who has lent us this city
in a covenant of grace,
enable us, through generosity of heart
and kindliness of intention,
to honour our side of the bargain
and in so doing embody a new relationship
between earth and heaven,
within which the city can become a safer place for
all people
to grow, thrive and flourish,
and in which the currency in every transaction
is the coinage of mercy, justice and peace.

Blessing   Bless the stressed,
bless the least,
bless the less,
bless the feast.

Bless the hype,
bless the tested,
bless the hope,
bless the vexed.

Bless the wild,
bless the pressed,
bless the child,
bless the mess.

Bless the strong,
bless the stretched,
bless the wrong,
bless the wretched.

Strangers

Adoration

Thank you, God, for the free city bus,
for the driver who whistles 'Stand up,
stand up for Jesus'
as we all lean round the corners.

Thank you for the seats that go lengthways,
so the lady in the burqa can smile at the toddler
in the pushchair
and the blind man can squeeze in beside her.

Thank you that the route takes in the university
and the man with blue hair has time to chat to the
lady with the trolley,
long enough to make her laugh.

Thank you that we go past the market,
so there is no need to carry
the snapper fish and plantains all the way up
the hill,
we can set our heavy bags down.

Thank you for the offers of seats,
even though it makes me feel old,
poles to hang on to when I am too proud
to accept,
mothers who sit children on knees.

Thank you for circles the bus makes all day,
arriving at the same stops, like a time-lapse film,
so that we always know one is on its way.

Thank you, God, for all the people that say
thank you
when they get on or off, or when they sit down.
Thank you for the regular blessing of the free city
bus, every ten minutes!

Confession

For giving too little,
for giving short shrift,
for giving no room,
for giving out lies.

For going too seldom,
for going too far,
for going too often,
for going too soon.

For getting too jumpy,
for getting too much,
for getting ill-tempered,
for getting unwise.

We ask for forgiveness,
but not to forget.
We ask to start over,
we ask for fresh eyes.

Absolution

For all the times we have given abundantly,
given space, told the truth, reigned ourselves in,
been pleasant and laughed,
thank you, that your forgiveness has been there
all along!

Intercession

We pray for all strangers in the city:
for incomers, immigrants and insurgents.

We pray for asylum seekers, refugees
and gypsies:
for those who fear for their lives or families.

We pray for people who feel strangers
to themselves:
for people who are transgendered or in the
process of coming out.

We pray for those who have never quite settled:
for wanderers and those troubled by mental
instability.

We pray for anyone who is restless or who has
run away:
for the ill at ease and the sick at heart.

We pray for people who have been trafficked
or sold:
for child prostitutes and the economically
imprisoned.

We pray for the restless and rootless in our city:
for the homeless and those who have
never belonged.

Commitment   May our city be as warm as hug,
as accepting as a lover,
as free-flowing as a river.

May our city be as hospitable as a mâitre de,
as tolerant as a grandfather,
as open as an outstretched hand.

May our city be as generous as a feast day,
as gentle as a soft landing,
as safe as a stronghold.

May our city be as creative as the Father,
as loving as the Saviour,
as flourishing as the Life-giver.

Blessing   Let this city be for sanctuary,
let this city be for inclusion,
may this city be for acceptance,
let this city be for everybody.
Amen.

New possibility

Adoration

Morning!
Light steps,
streets brushed ready.

Wake up!
Hopes raised,
like morning blinds.

Shoes bright!
New news,
traffic parted.

Fresh start,
clean paths,
clothed in promise!

Confession

God, the city is so cynical,
seen it all before somehow,
expecting nothing more.

Old hat city, a broken record of promises,
doubting anything better,
believing no news is good news.

But you came to bring us life,
in all its fullness and festivity,
to dislodge the dynasties of doubt.

You are a risen Christ,
crucified outside the walls
yet returning with the breath of spirit.

Risen within the urbane,
like new yeast, like effervescent wine,
as a new companion on the road.

Rise on these confusing days,
kick-start the urban dream,
pierce the city's bubble.

Lift us up, God, trouble us,
like a song whistled
on a busy street on a rain-soaked day.

Absolution   There is the rumour of good news
within these walls,
a hint that God is stirring up a rising
in protest at the complacence of the status quo.

A summons:
'Start over,
pick up your cross,
believe me,
arise, it can be done!'

Intercession   We pray for the rising of this city to new heights,
we pray for the transformation of this city to
new sight,
we pray for the deepening of this city to
new depths,
we pray for keeping of this city in true light.

We pray for the upholding of this city in
new trust,
we pray for the raising of this city in new hope,
we pray for the freeing of this city in new truth,
we pray for the voicing of the city in few words.

We pray for the changing of the city in
new dreams,
we pray for the releasing of the city to new choice,
we pray for the liberation of this city to new love,
we pray for the resurrection of the city in
due time.

Commitment

Risen Christ, I will not cling to you,
I will walk lightly with my faith
and be prepared to be surprised.

Risen Christ, I will not cling to you,
I will not seek your name
but only your curious company at every turn.

Risen Christ, I will not cling to you,
I will wait in this city for your insight
to inspire a deeper vision of your grace.

Risen Christ, I will not cling to you,
I will roll away the boulders of doubt
and find your love unwrapped.

Risen Christ, I will not cling to you,
I will walk light-stepped,
assured of your risen mystery.

Blessing

In my coming and going,
in my doubt and believing,
in my sleeping and rising,
in my dying and grieving.

In my to-ing and fro-ing,
in my clinging and cleaving,
in my keeping and crying,
in my rising and leaving.

Be my love and my living,
be my soulmate and stranger,
be my grasping and giving,
be my peace within danger.

Be my start and my finish,
be my leaving and homing,
be my wholeness and struggle,
be my life and becoming.

Rage

Adoration

Exciting city, enticing city,
inviting city, involving city,
enraging city, endearing city,
confusing city, confining city,
aggressive city, transgressive city,
alarming city, disarming city,
wealthy city, unhealthy city,
envious city, devious city,
impressive city, depressive city,
addictive city, contradictive city,
tricking city, wicked city,
infernal city, eternal city.

Confession

The people are rising up in anger,
they have been imprisoned by dictators,
their patience is broken,
they stand in solidarity with each other,
they are resisting the bullets,
the soldiers are neighbours disguised as enemies,
their uniforms have smothered their mercy.

The city is on fire with rage,
it bursts out in flames of fury,
which engulf the streets,
the mob is a roaring dragon, unleashing
its breath,
its nostrils flare like furnaces,
its vicious tongue swipes the children from
the path,
it has a tail of retaliation.

The people seek justice, they will seize it by force,
their tempers have lost their reason,
they are intent on revenge,
there is no holding the crowd, it cannot be kettled,*
its desire is all-consuming,
it will sweep the city clean with its wrath,
the powerful will submit to its thrust.

Absolution

If your rage is for justice,
and your passion is for mercy,
then go in peace.

Intercession

We pray for those who say 'NO MORE',
we pray for those who say 'NO LESS',
we pray for those who make no sound,
we pray for those whose hearts protest,
we pray for those who say 'NOT NOW',
we pray for those who say 'NOT EVER',
we pray for those who keep their peace,
we pray for those where quiet is better,
we pray for those who say 'NO WAR',
we pray for those who say 'NO DEATH',
we pray for those who seek release,
we pray for those who face the test,
we pray for those who say 'NOT THAT',
we pray for those who say 'NO NEVER',
we pray for those who hold their ground,
we pray for those who find no rest,
we pray for those who say 'NOT ME',
we pray for those who say 'NOT THEM',
we pray for those who keep no score,
in order that the poor are blessed.

* This is the term used for the process by which police control crowds in riot situations.

Commitment

I will not give tit for tat,
I will not give eye for eye,
I will not trade lie for truth,
I will not trade tooth for tooth.

I will turn the other cheek,
I will go the extra mile,
I will take the heavy load,
I will bear the weighty cross.

I will wear the crown of shame,
I will feel the nails of hate,
I will bear the name of love,
I will give my all for that.

Blessing

May the God of wrath and righteousness
fill the city with holy anger,
tempered with mercy.

Green

Ordinary time, extraordinary God

In the Church's calendar, green signifies 'ordinary times' which fill in the gaps between the high seasons or the penitential ones. In an urban context this all gets mixed up, so that we live both an ordinary and an extraordinary reality at the same time. In this section I want to think about how ordinary life is suffused by the incarnate God, and how in the city we are often called upon to discern the work of God amongst what on the surface might appear drab or dreary.

I think about the shades that the city wears, the greyness of much around us, and I perceive how this reality can soften our visual landscape and blur the edges. I reflect on how we can be preoccupied by glamour and colour and forget to rejoice in the unspectacular everyday nature of God. I pray for anyone who lives in a dark place, within themselves or in the built environment and ask the breath of the gentle spirit of God to blow a new understanding into the daily process of being alive.

I enjoyed writing prayers about 'deliveries' because I found all kinds of meanings in the word that I had not anticipated. I thought of the dawn being delivered onto 'the belly of night' and the postmen bringing news and terse demands. I realised that in the city people often fail to deliver what is promised and there is a large amount of political fiction delivered by people in power. I was reminded of the deliveries that I have known, and what I have been delivered from and I asked God afresh to deliver me from greed and for the blessing of simplicity.

In the next set of prayers I explored how many people travel around the city with no name. I pondered anonymity both as alienation and a blessing. I realised how careless we can be with our names, and with those of other people. I recalled that God calls us each by names, and that we are both known and a mystery.

Commuting is part of many people's daily experience in the city. I tried to give a new take on the experience, seeing the ebb and flow of the city to be life-giving. I critiqued my own experience of commuting and realised the extent of my silent judgements on fellow travellers and asked God for a new commitment to being process- rather than outcome-driven.

Finally I took an overdue look at green as an environmental theme, realising that our care of the city environment is also an everyday task. I had some fun, revisiting an old fairy tale before returning to the vision of Revelation and imagining a new city where the people could flourish anew.

Shades of grey

Adoration

Charcoal of granite,
lichen-etched statues,
grizzled cloud cushions.

Above the gravestones,
skeins of geese homing,
thoughts like swift shadows.

Black and white merging,
rubbed by a blurred thumb,
gentling opposites.

Indecisive smoke,
merging of viewpoints,
opposites meeting.

The city's headscarf,
veiling cathedrals,
voile of gentleness.

Ash, dusty doorways,
webs on gutter turns,
tensile persistence.

Jets' fleeting sketch trails,
mute fuzz of street lamps,
the slowing of fog.

Boiling urn steaming,
eyes circled with mist,
silver curls wisping.

River reflections,
concrete joists crane high,
the steel of the bridge.

Coins in a deep well,
veins bubbling old hands,
dusk's calm reverie.

She's a wise city,
tempered by gentleness,
silvered by twilight.

Confession

It seems I have been preoccupied by colour,
by celebrity and glamour.
I have dreamed of youth and recognition,
forgetting possibilities of greys.

It seems I have been intent on being jolly,
resenting routine rhythms.
I have lived superficially,
overlooking the steady gift of days.

It seems I have strived to solve dilemmas,
rather than holding fast with them.
I have tried to make things better,
considering illness as a passing phase.

It seems I have endeavoured to buy contentment,
seduced by bargains, things I didn't need.
I have searched only for cheap treasure,
forgetting how the routine can amaze.

It seems I have courted the spectacular,
longing for highs of holiness and joy.
I have had my eyes set on the horizon
and overlooked the daily round of grace.

Absolution

To be with God, is to be totally ordinary and
totally loved,
this is the miracle of incarnation,
it is the miracle of life,
Jesus says, 'Live!'

And as I am forgiven all the above and more
besides,
I will live, with joy and gratitude, fired up by rage
and glory,
content with who I am and all my failings,
held in the loving view of grace.

Behold, all things are new,
I am new,
there is nothing left to regret.

Intercession

This is a prayer for anyone who is depressed,
whose experience or memories cast dark shadows
over their lives,
for those who cannot lift themselves
out of despair.

This prayer
is our prayer.

This prayer is for anyone who lives in a place
without sunlight,
whose relationships are hopeless or abusive
or gone,
for those who cannot envisage tomorrow.

This prayer
is our prayer.

This prayer is for anyone who feels closed down
by life,
who has not got the energy either to continue
or to make changes,
for those who are exhausted or have run out
of steam.

This prayer
is our prayer.

This prayer is for anyone who has negative voices
in their head,
who is fraught with contradictions and
uncertainty,
for those who cannot feel forgiven or free.

This prayer
is our prayer.

This prayer is for the bored, the listless and
the perplexed,
who feel stuck in cycles of negativity or poverty,
for those who sense they are grounded
or imprisoned.

This prayer
is our prayer.

These prayers are for all of us,
who in this city are more together than we
are apart,
for a fresh sense of purpose and unity.

This prayer
is our prayer.

This is a prayer for our city,
that even within the grey and the perplexing,
we may learn to sing whilst it is yet dark.

This prayer
is our prayer.

Commitment   Gentle breath of the Spirit of God:
if I may be more forthright
put the wind into my sails,
if I may be more humble
take the wind out.

If I may be more impulsive
put the wind into my sails,
if I may be more patient
take the wind out.

If I may be more passionate
put the wind into my sails,
if I may be more considered
take the wind out.

If I may be more outspoken
put the wind into my sails,
if I may be more silent
take the wind out.

If I may be more upbeat
put the wind into my sails,
if I may be more tranquil
take the wind out.

Breathe through me,
breathe from me,
breathe within me,
breathe beyond me.

May my in-breath be for your wisdom,
may my out-breath be for your glory.

Blessing   Twilight God,
grey God,
pondering God,
bless us slowly,
bless us wisely,
bless us gently.
Amen.

Deliveries

Adoration

The dawn is delivered onto the belly of night,
the milk on the rattling float chimes lauds,
the city colours, with its first breath.

The wagons' airbrakes hiss matins,
armfuls of flowers packed, like cradled infants,
buds of celebration and pardon.

Barrels of beer rolled across cobbles,
dropped into cellars by heavy-handed drivers,
anticipating the small hours.

Then the bread, baked warmly ready for
sandwiches,
the young women with plastic gloves,
slicing and sectioning the noonday lunch.

Parcels, postmen in shorts, bicycles,
laden with news, terse demands,
postcards from secretaries, invoices.

The heavy theatre wagon, labouring up the
side street,
stage-door transactions, scenery, props,
elderly actors rehearse green room vespers.

Once the students are loaded onto the last bus
the day dies in the arms of the night,
compline, the last rites, the offices of dusk.

Confession

Too often the city fails to deliver its manifestos,
it squanders its vision for short-term objectives,
qualifying generosity with financial constraints.

Too often the city has not delivered its citizens,
from being possessed by desires,
spoken and hidden, fanciful and frightening.

Too often the city has delivered empty speeches,
rhetoric of fantasies, political fictions,
the empty words of false hope.

Absolution

Midwife God, deliver us from stillborn promises,
bring us new life, fresh hope, new beginnings,
show us that we are not defined by our past but
called into the future
and show us the way a city can be a totally
wonderful and wholesome place.

And within this vision, reassure us that you are
present in all the muddle and mess.
We can never alienate ourselves from your love
and we can never be distanced from your grace
and joy.

Jesus says, 'I come to bring life, and life in all
its fullness.'

Thank you, Jesus!

Intercession

For all people who bring post, for parcel van
drivers and couriers,
for all pizza deliverers, takeaway drivers and
veg-box companies,
for all laundry collectors, ironing and
dry cleaning services,
for all supermarket deliveries, mobile shops
and fish vans,

for all replenishers of soap dispensers,
vending machines and water stations,
for all midwives, health visitors, district nurses
and breastfeeding advisors,
for all deliveries, for all deliverers,
for all deliverance
we pray.

Commitment   If I forfeit the cloak,
if I leave the safe boat,
if I proffer the cheek,
if I carry the load.

If I honour the meek,
if I travel the road,
if I discount the cost,
if I journey the mile.

If I pity the lost,
if I challenge the strong,
if I offer the coat,
if to Christ I belong.

Then the coat and the cloak
and the mile and the cost,
I will give and give gladly
in search of the lost.

Blessing   May the blessing of simplicity,
deliver this city from greed.
May the blessing of peacefulness,
deliver this city from bloodshed.

May the blessing of honesty
deliver this city from corruption.
May the blessing of thankfulness
deliver this city from selfishness.

May the blessing of God,
Creator, Deliverer, Inspirer,
fill this city with life, laughter and hopefulness.
Amen.

Anonymity

Adoration

God of a thousand names,
yet mystery,
God of the everyday,
yet beyond,
God of revelation,
yet unknown,
praise you,
for this named,
yet mysterious city,
that it belongs,
that it is known,
and yet to be discovered.

Confession

We have traded names like commodities,
sold databases and mailing lists.
We have told tales on celebrities
and gossiped the scandals of the rich.

We have seen the poor as issues
and forgotten their humanity,
hoped they would disappear,
rather than identify their need.

We have herded people into statistics,
we have kettled* faceless crowds,
used names as a tool for form filling,
overlooking that they are a gift from you.

We ask for forgiveness for our carelessness,
for prying and intrusive fascinations,
for taking names, for calling names,
rather than waiting for names to be given.

* This is the term used for the process by which police control crowds in riot situations.

Absolution   God calls us and recalls us: to our true identity,
he has called us to live our own names,
this is our vocation, to live out our unique being,
to be distinctly ourselves.
Through this simple truth, we are liberated,
God has called us by our name,
we are his.

Intercession   How do we pray for the city, when so much
is hidden,
how do we pray for the neighbours whose
language we don't share,
how do we raise up the complicated issues
of strangers,
how do our best intentions include the
nameless ones,
how do we honour the patterns of other faiths,
how do we challenge issues without racism,
how do we love the shouters and ranters
of the night,
how can we transform the city's bad name,
how do we name the God of justice,
how do we name the cry for peace,
how do we name the issues that are wicked,
how do we challenge patterns of neglect,
when the answers feel beyond us,
when the issues seem too complex,
when we feel powerless and afraid,
when we are unable to pray?

Pray through us, God,
pray into the questions of the city,
pray gently,
pray strongly.

Commitment   The challenge of living here is my challenge,
I will rise to it in the morning,
I will bear with it at night.

The challenge of this city is our challenge,
we will rise to it in the morning,
we will bear with it at night.

The challenge of city living is the world's
challenge,
the sun will rise to it in the morning,
the moon will bear with it at night.

Being here is the Earth's challenge,
God will bear with her at nightfall,
and rise with her at first light.

Blessing   We live within the name of God,
who creates us,
who cherishes us,
who encompasses us,
who holds us,
who sustains us,
who remembers us.
Amen.

Commuting

Adoration   Praise be to God for the seven forty-two,
for the seats with the table
and functioning loo.

Thanks be to God for the daily commute,
for the mobile signal,
reliable route.

Bless the creator of signals and track,
the coffee, the trolley,
the overhead rack.

For the sleepers and rails,
the stewards,
inspectors,
cleaners,
maintainers,
and ticket collectors.

Blessings to God for the mobile reception,
the wi-fi provision,
waste paper collection.

If I get in a frenzy because of delays,
may the time I am wasting
be used for God's praise.

Confession

If I sit on the train making judgements
about the man complaining about his bonuses
and the woman rubbishing her boss,
if I am the silent judge of this compartment,
inwardly despising the lads sinking the lager,
the executive mum talking to her kids by mobile,
if I am the invisible critic
of all my superficial perceptions,
then remind me God that
when the Underground was blown up,
it was people like this who took off their coats
and held the hands of the dying and distraught,
who waited for the emergency services,
resisted their own need for safety –
and I wonder, would I have done the same?

You just can't get the stereotypes these days,
and I am sorry, God, for seeing people
superficially,
as if I was a detached spectator on the world.

Absolution

Incarnate God, with us in person,
in the everyday Jesus, in our neighbour,
thank you that you know us inwardly
and continually love us into new perceptions.

Intercession

We pray for people who are neither here
nor there,
don't know if they are coming or going,
who have lost track of who they are,

for people in transition between jobs,
between relationships,
between destinations,

for people delayed,
in a jam
or up in the air,

waiting for a signature,
a payment,
for completion.

We pray, loving God, for the ebb and flow of
this city,
that daily journeys will be continually blessed
with humour, patience and shared humanity.

Commitment   We commit ourselves to being outcome-light and
process-rich,
to being less concerned with our success and
more with our way of being.

We commit ourselves to trusting the process
of transformation,
to being less concerned with outer changes and
more with our way of relating.

We commit ourselves to journeying openly
and lovingly,
to being less concerned with reaching our
destination and more with our way of travelling.

Blessing   God of the shorelines and edges,
bless the betwixt and between people,
bless the cracks and fissures,
the hopes and waiting,
bless the journeys as well as the arrival.
Amen.

Environment

Adoration

Early blackbird heralds the street light dawn,
rattling the bin, the night fox scatters
a mess of pickings on the pavement.

Tap, tap, the rain from the broken downspout,
hungry rat trips the trap, frees the cheese,
high squirrel trapezes the branches.

Scavenger magpie chatters a chiding,
under the canal's skim the grebe darts,
half-submerged, the brown vole trawls the bank.

Silently the grass grows in the gutter,
rooks gleaning a nest for the chimney,
busy pigeons clean chips from platforms.

Fragile city restoring her balance,
alive to the smallest of creatures,
like a hen gathering her chickens.

Confession

This is the city that Jack built.
This is the soil, rich and wet,
that lay under the city that Jack built.
This is the digger, yellow and loud,
that scooped up the soil, rich and wet,
that lay under the city that Jack built.
This is the worm, red and fat,
that lay in the soil, rich and wet,
that the digger scooped out, yellow and loud,
from under the city that Jack built.
This is the concrete, grey and hard,
that went into the hole, dark and deep,
that the digger scooped out, yellow and loud,
to make the foundations, safe and strong,
under the city that Jack built.

This is the building, shiny and new, with its glass
so bright and clear,
that shone in the city, proud and tall,
the mighty city that Jack built.
This is the bird that fashioned a nest
in the roof of the building, shiny and new,
at the heart of the city that Jack built.
This is the chick that needs the worm,
this is the worm, dead and dry,
that lies on the soil, parched as dust,
scooped out by the digger, yellow and loud,
around the building, safe and strong,
in the mighty city that Jack built.

Absolution

In the city of God
the leaves of the trees are for the healing
of the nations.
In the cracks around us and despite us
the rising sap of nature takes root and brings life.
Through this cycle of creation we are also
made new,
not by our own efforts but by the forgiveness
inherent in creation.

Praise God that our new life does not depend
on us
and that a fresh start is already underway.

Intercession

We bring to God the city's ecosystems,
the balance of the natural and built environments.

We pray for the integrity of Creation, natural and
humanly made,
a sense of tenderness for the plants and creatures
in the cracks of the city.

We ask for a new sense of honour for the city,
a respect for its webs of life,
that we may all flourish together
without destruction.

We long to be mindful of the city's reliance on the
countryside for recreation and space,
and pray for a new respect for those who farm
or maintain the land.

We offer to God our desire to reduce our carbon
footprints and to use less energy,
asking for a spirit of conservation both by
ordinary people and policy makers.

We pray that the city will be a green place,
that the air and water will be clean,
and a healthy environment sustained for
all creation.

Commitment

I commit myself to simpler living,
to desiring less,
recycling more.

I commit myself to ethical shopping,
to sourcing goods wisely,
opting for fair trade.

I commit myself to just economics,
to reducing world debt,
boycotting unjust practices.

I commit myself to empowering politics,
to sharing resources,
reducing the gap between rich and poor.

Blessing

May the creatures of the city remind us of
the Creator,
may the water of the city bring a new freedom,
may the air of the city, breathe the Spirit's energy,
may the city flourish
with life in all its fullness.
Amen.

Incarnation

This final gathering of prayers for the city focuses on particular groups of people and their lived experience within the urban context. I reflect on what it means to survive, and how liturgy is often skewed to favour the voices of the powerful. I think about the 'coming-out people' and the need to listen to their experience of transformation. I ponder what it means to let go, to leave the city and to move on. And finally I get to one of my favourite Bible stories, the Road to Emmaus, during which Jesus falls into step with the disciples, bringing new hope and causing them to return to Jerusalem.

In all these prayers my longing is that we begin to see the city with fresh eyes, that we will return to it again and again, and be encouraged to discover the incarnate God, walking the streets with us and bringing life and love.

Prayers for the surviving people

No searching or knowing, please

Lord, I don't want you to search me and
know me,
or understand my thoughts afar off,
I would prefer it if you didn't knit me together
at all,
or follow me down to the depths of the sea.
Whilst we're being honest, it would help me if
I didn't have to call you 'Lord',
also, please stand a long way away,
well out of my personal space,
no rendezvous up on the wings of the morning.

I seriously don't want to be touched by you,
definitely don't lay hands on me at any time,
certainly not without asking.
I don't even want to be in your palm,
or the apple of your eye,
in fact, I would prefer it if we dumped the body
stuff altogether.

If we do manage to have a conversation
some time,
there are some ground rules,
'No smiting' comes top of the list.
I will be standing up, not kneeling or doing
anything with upturned hands,
definitely no supplication or begging or any other
sort of grovelling from me.
Your body language is a matter of choice
but no 'coming down from on high'.

I'd like to talk with you at some point,
it might be hard for you to hear what I
have to say,
but presumably you're big enough to take it?

We come shrouded in strange silences

We come shrouded in strange silences,
we are bound by overwhelming confusions,
our desires have been veiled in secrecy,
our bodies entombed,
our senses numb,
our voices muffled.
We ask, 'Can we go on?'
We ask, 'Why hasn't Jesus come to us?'

Where is rescue, God of absence?
How will you save us from the fears that stifle us,
from the terrors of visitations that come
in darkness,
from the dread of revelations that come
in daylight?

Will we ever hear you calling us from the
dark tomb,
longing for us to come back to life,
to sit and eat at your table,
before we have washed, before we are acceptable,
tearing ourselves free from the things that bind us,
letting our bodies and our stories
be brought to light?

We come shrouded by strange silences,
O God, call us back to life.

The wounded company of the unlikely

So, there they gathered,
a man deaf from birth
alongside the weary tax consultant,
the woman with secret shames,
the little girl whose granny died of AIDS,
a homeless guy, once left for dead, limping,
alongside the poor-sighted priest.
They had bread to share, ingredients,
effort, sleepless nights.
They brought news that demons could be laid
to rest,
stones need not be thrown,
a surprising freedom could be found
alongside this wounded company
of the unlikely.

I am choosing to remember in another way

I am choosing to remember
in another way,
raise the curtain,
today I'm centre stage;
that was just Act One
of an unfinished play.
It is time to change this age-old script,
to put the guilty villain to a certain death.
I'm not an object in this shameful narrative,
part of the scenery, hidden by the gauze;
it is my day to take a bow.
So turn the page, prepare for a surprise,
because, right now, I'm drawing breath.
I'm going to rise and proclaim who I am:
the leading lady, ME.
I'm going to be the principal
of Acts Two and Three!

Prayers for the 'coming-out people'

I am

I am not what I thought I was,
I am not who they think I am,
I am not where I want to be,
I am not.

I might be someone else,
I might be somewhat different,
I might be something more,
I might be.

I could be really changed,
I could be much more open,
I could be glad of myself,
I could be.

I am who you see,
I am where I need to be,
I am who I think I am,
I am!

Coming-out city

May this city be blessed by prophets
who see a different path,
where prosperity is about peace,
not finance,
and justice soars above the rooftops
as an eagle.

May this city be blessed with imagination,
where old men see visions of transformation,
young women draw up good plans
for our streets

and freedom falls into step
with the broken.

May this city live its own name boldly,
released from competition and conformity,
so that all people will flourish
in their own bodies
and peace be broadcast
like good news.

You will call me names

You will call me names,
I will call you blessed.
You will draw a line,
I will draw a breath.
You will take a stone,
I will take a moment.
You will see me barred,
I will see it through.
You will hold your peace,
I will hold your hand.
You will keep me in,
I will be coming out.

God of the 'coming-out people'

God of the coming-out people,
bless all those who are frightened to
be themselves,
who must face their own inner assumptions,
as well as those of families and friends.

Bless those who face disappointments,
who are ridiculed or disregarded
because of orientation or disability,
as well as those who find these changes
confusing.

God of all transformations,
give courage to all people who are muddled,
struggling or afraid about who they are
becoming,
bless them with hope and resilience.

God who is faithful to us,
even when our faith and identity disintegrate,
bring the coming-out people close to you,
to discover true identity in your company.

I am who I am, God!

I am who I am, God,
and that's a fact!
I am who I am, God,
and that's a mystery!

Prayers for the 'letting-go people'

Lost!

Three days your mother searched,
finding you alive,
listening.

Only then could you speak with authority,
of lost coins,
of lost sons,
of lost sheep,
of lost hope,
of pearls of great price,
of buried talents,
of a city that had forfeited its way,
of a seed buried in the earth,
and in the end, lost again.

Three days your mother searched,
finding you alive,
listening.

Remembrance Sunday

At this cenotaph
I stand implicated
in warfare I have not committed,
in conflict I have never seen.

I carry my involvement
as red as a poppy,
as weighty as a silence,
as sharp as a sword.

For I have joined
in blaming others,
in constraining others.
in reducing others.

It is not that
I have forgotten,
that I never realised
or that I turned a blind eye.

But rather that I failed to remember
that my enemy is my brother,
the 'terrorist' is my sister
and that God is the Father of us all.

Leaving the city

As I leave this city
I give its streets and pavements
into the ways of God,
the pathfinder.

As I leave this city
I give its openings and opportunities
thankfully to God,
the gatekeeper.

As I leave this city
I say goodbye to its threats and tensions,
offering my struggles to God,
the peacemaker.

As I leave this city
I let go of the pressure and striving,
releasing the stress to God,
the timekeeper.

As the tide turns
and I leave this beloved city,
I give this place into the hands of God,
the night watchman.

Paths of faithfulness

God of the city,
you may brush off the dust
but you also wash tired feet.
Your feet are nailed to a cross
and yet you walk with disciples to Emmaus.
Give us the feet of faithfulness,
to go with you as you do with us,
walking pavements of blessing
and alleyways of joy.

Prayers for the hopeful people

I have seen

I have seen the park keeper, sweeping,
up to his ankles in autumn,
the leaves rise in swirling gusts
russet, as a bronzed bracelet.

The park is crisped with frost,
an urban shoreline
between the tides of work and home;
the park keeper has a small fire lit.

Unusual to see a park keeper,
I thought they had been abolished
cut by the councils like the branches
that burn to charcoal in the breeze.

The trees are unwrapped now
for winter, yet somehow
more majestic in their starkness,
resilient for the storms to come.

They have shaken off their foliage
free, storing their strength for budding,
their own mulch to nourish them,
swept in copper piles around their roots.

We had hoped

We had hoped that the banks would take
fewer bonuses.
We had hoped that Top Shop would pay their tax.
We had hoped that the army would come home.
We had hoped the nuclear programme
would be cut.
We had hoped there would be a cap on credit.
We had hoped the libraries would not be closed.
We had hoped the free bus would stay running.
We had hoped the carers would keep their jobs.
We had hoped that the walls would be
taken down.
We had hoped that ordinary people would topple
the dictators.
We had hoped that the women would not have
been evicted.
We had hoped that the refugees would have leave
to stay.

But we did not really believe it was possible,
and we left before we had seen things through,
we set off for our homes, to find comfort,
we thought there was no point hanging around.

Hoping

Even as you are leaving
I fall into step beside you,
soon you will hope differently,
despair will be broken,
like fresh bread.

Remembering

When the complexities of the city are too
hard to fathom,
and the decisions made by those in power
seem senseless,
when we walk away,
walk beside us.

When our hopes are confounded by distant
authorities
and the needs of the poorest are overlooked,
when we walk away,
walk beside us.

When we can see no place for conscience
and the city seems to be consumed by crowds,
when we walk away,
walk beside us.

When the city is faithless to its common purpose
and commercialism drives the agenda,
when we walk away,
walk beside us.

When the struggling are betrayed
and our hopes for a better way have been
demolished,
when we walk away,
walk beside us.

When hope seems to have been crucified
and there seems no point in remaining,
when we walk away,
walk beside us.

Longing

Break the bread with us, Jesus,
show us our place in the story,
open our eyes to a new meaning,
bring us to the table of understanding.

And we will return to the city gladly,
proclaiming that you have risen,
we will share more than crusts with strangers
and bring hope in our stride.

For you have taken a place at the table,
with the broken and hopeless,
opened our eyes to a way of feasting
that is merciful and just.

Come, sit, share the eucharist
of hope for the city, turn us
on our heels of doubt,
invite us, feed us, raise us!

Blessing

May the God of Creation
fall into step with this city,
so that all who live here
will be opened
to their place in the story of God.
Amen.

Prayer for feasts

God of ordinary things,
washing, drying up, missing the last bus home,
move us continuously to
marvel at everyday liturgies,
rainbows in bubbles, wobbly teeth,
the flavours of cheese.
Help us to hear the intercession
within commonplace words of love:
'Have a great day', 'Be safe',
'Come home soon.'
Encourage us to hear the psalms of friendship
at bedsides,
litanies of longing in the shadows of grief.
Celebrate your Eucharist of living
in the routine rituals of unremarkable days.